Meridian of Life

Michelle Caddy

Presentation by *BookLeaf Publishing*

Web: www.bookleafpub.com

E-mail: info@bookleafpub.com

ISBN: 9789357442435

First edition 2023

*Dedicated to Little Michelle who I now treat
with love and compassion.*

PREFACE

Simply, this book of poems is about taking some risks, seeing if I could get onto paper, into words, the things that are on my mind: ageing, identity, time, pain, joy, Hamlet and Joni Mitchell.

Palmate

Five from one reach out
Lobes of smashed green and orange
The autumn waving.

Gothel

Without beauty, dust.
A woman of a 'certain age'
Grapples with the irony of new lines, a new
body, a
New, yet old existence which is
Existing, only just.

A fragile ego feeds her the story.
Be gazed upon or begone
From sight
From passion
From energy
From belonging
From allowing
Yourself

A fragile ego that will gobble you all up
Lives that truth
In every bit of angst at the sight of
Lost hair in the shower
Lost bounce in the eyelids
Lost belief
Lost.

Mother Gothel, mother substitute
Her mothering, smothering.
Feeds you on her breast of abject sustenance that
is a
Addictive, reductive, destructive black green
troll gaze.
Feeds on the surface, cares only for sur
face.

Doggedness Dogginess

Agreed: there are many things that are just pure
joy.
You can think of your own
And disagree with the lists of others.
But
Can we all agree that there is undeniable joy in
the
Frequent phenomenon of dog-owner symmetry?

A little something in the fur/hair that matches
Texture or hue.
Matched energy, seen or heard in the bounding
or the plodding along (doggedly).

Twin snouts
Pace and gait
The same dart in the eyes, sometimes matching
jackets.

Going for walk is now a game of dog-owner
snap.
An aged pigeon-toed bulldog, utterly pissed off
at this stroll appears first and then
The owner, rotund belly, jowly and gruff.
Nothing but joy for me in this human-canine
overlap.

Function of Dysfunction

Don't let anyone tell you that
Trauma doesn't serve any function.
Oh yes, it will do its work
Until you have to do 'the work'.
Meanwhile the shit you do reserves
The right to reign over 'you'
Like there is 'you' that is even real.
Unfettered
Unconditioned
Free of the group think, ostracised.
So say nothing
So do nothing
Don't get pregant
Don't tell your father
Say nothing
Do nothing, be nothing.
Believe for decades that you are nothing.
Apologise
Be good
Be silent
Be
Un-be
Re-be
Learn some shattering truths that lift the
Veil away from the 'truth' you've been fed

Family is all that matters, this
Truth you have clung to like it's oxygen
Truth that chokes the fucking life from you.

A hand, fingers outstretched, hovering inches
From your face, so you can see but not see
Clearly enough to function without dysfunction.

And when that hand, outstretched fingers moves
You realise in choking grief that it's
Your hand.
You are blocking you.
Dysfunction has been functioning
Until you finally malfunction.

And then, oh boy
Do you sometimes miss your old settings.
Late at night
Doubting yourself, as you reset yourself, finding
yourself.

Winter-Spring

7

Dark clinging at dawn
Wisps of spring, life returning
Lemon light of morn.

J.M. Heart Song

Caramel bell voice that exposes the hurt.

I picture her in silhouette, her owl eyes

Seeing the depth of things that

Benignly exist, Nature's gifts and wonders

That live for her, as energy, as love.

The hurt, laid bare in her lines of

the frailties of humanity:

Entitlement, ego, avarice.

Vicious growth gains on her too.

Tempers the sweet to create her truth.

Her heart song.

Angst in Ageing

At my age, you'd think all angst would go.
Not so.
Panic barrels into me with zeal as I spot one
more line.
Notice a drooping, tissue thinning
Under this lotioned hand of mine.

It's not about the looks you see, it's really not.
It's the hard lesson learning that time does as its
own thing
This is all you've got
And you're barely surviving.

A wake up call would be sweet.
Sweetly welcomed in and held in relief.
Knee-jerk, Teflon-coated me would deflect,
Minimise myself, never miss a beat.

Right now, it's all a type of grief.

JOMO (Joy of Missing Out)

The FOMO ages into the JOMO.
There is joy in not having to
Choose an outfit
Realise you no longer have outfits so need to
Shop for an outfit
Make small talk
Discuss political u-turns, scandals and faux pas
Queue in the cold, quickly sobering up and
Seeing the once alluring spaces of beer and
vomit.
An abject reminder of what
You once feared to miss out on.

Greatness

My children are greatness.
Pure hearts.
Bracing honesty.
Fragile sensitivity at minutiae
Unfelt to most.

Their greatness has lessons.
Unlearning of the ways we've always done it.
Without the shadows of all the egos, they
subvert and revolt.
Saying 'this does not work for me'
Expressed boldly.

Until those shadows start to creep and
Apologies begin to be offered
Sorry for being me
Sorry for being true
Sorry for being so confronting to you in
My Greatness.

The Newborn Scrunch

What does it say?

I am not ready to unfold to the world.

I am unabashedly in my body.

I am tentatively checking where I end and you begin.

I am ready to be held in love.

Hold me around my heart.

Cycle Breaker

I will speak my truth
Risk the known and unknown fear
Live unveiled and bruised.

Hamlet

14

Hamlet the Tempest
He was mad but north-north west
Knew his own mind best.

Dissociation

15

The lines don't flow the way I imagined.
Lyricism dodges me
So my thoughts come at me dart-like
Efficient and mean.

Losing people, losing status, losing self.
You would think poetry would
Spill out of me in waves of
Beautiful dark imagery.

But in place of that it is
Knock on wood.
Nothing.
Feelings stay buried
Staring into space
Unable to recall.

Beyond this blur, association is going to charge
in.
It will sting
It will churn
It will attach
It will remind me to feel, switch me back
To life.

Mouse

A pet name for a little pet
A little pet who remains quiet
Who remains quiet, always observing
Always observing, keeping herself safe
Keeping herself safe doesn't always work
Doesn't always work when a punching bag is
needed
When a punching bag is needed all the
Resentment and fragility come out to play
Come out to play with the threat of the belt
The threat of the belt and the truth of the hand
The truth of hand and the other holding
The other holding you down to be hit
To be hit over and over in silence
In silence you wait for her to tire
You wait for her to tire then retreat
Then retreat to your top bunk belly down
Belly down to spare your throbbing legs
Your throbbing legs tuck in and up
Tuck in and up and then you allow the cry
You allow the cry to come but still so quiet
So quiet you lie hearing him approach
Hearing him approach, reach over and give
you a Penguin biscuit
A Penguin biscuit you will nibble

You will nibble
Nibble like a mouse.

Birth Order

You are seven minutes apart
You are shorter than her
You weighed less than her
You had fairer hair then her.

A little behind
A little below
A little less
A little paler.

The sharing of a birthday card.
Improper twins that had to match
For Mother's supply.

Imagine insisting you are who you say
You are and have someone say no,
You are her.

Never ending comparison living inside twin bias
That blinds people to singularity.

Seen

It was a look in his eye
A flash of the lightest blue
That said

I see you.

Absence-Presence

Very often, said so casually, so universally
'Remember having birthday parties as a kid?'
No. No is my answer.
Birthdays tinged with a simmering resentment of
obligation.
All the outward trappings present
Cake
Gifts
A party tea
A present for a sibling
So she is not left out
Despite the sharing of self you already do.

But no guests.
An absence of others to
Celebrate you and
You alone.

An exhausting performance in gratitude.

Shadow

21

She scares me to death
Resentful avoidant bitch
Frightened and fragile.

Disclaimer

This is not saying I regret my children.

It happens so insidiously

The erasure of your heart self.

Your needs fall away as

You embody the expectations of

Mother m(other)

Throw in some disability to really seal the deal.

Isolate for self-preservation.

Clothe yourself in martyr's robes so you

Have SOME identity.

If you're lucky the veil will slip

And you will unlearn this bullshit that

Keeps you at the bottom.

Things I love/a list

Blackbirds
Brooding grey skies over oceans
Morning light
My sons being together, unaware we are
watching
Autistic honesty
A triple crown
Creme brulee
Malaprops
The itch relief of an cotton earbud
Line dried laundry
That first coffee
Stretching
Late night soul talks
Madonna
Crocuses
Showing my love in the form of hugs
Tweezers
Lists!

They just are

Evolution tells us, insists even that we
Human beings are the most evolved
Superior species on the planet.

Why is it then, that in my immobile despair
My panic at the world, my heaviness at waking
That I envy a seagull atop a roof?

They're never in their own heads, stuck.
They 're never lost.
They don't give a fuck.
They just are.

Milton Keynes UK
Ingram Content Group UK Ltd.
UKHW020733290923
429627UK00017B/921